Hoo Knew?!

By **Bob Baumert**

Illustrated by **Mark Bockrath**

ISBN: 978-1-939237-95-8

Illustrations by Mark Bockrath

Published by Suncoast Digital Press, Inc.
Sarasota, Florida, USA

Dedicated to my current and future grandchildren.

I hope you enjoy this little bit of fun!

Did you, too, know those two

down by St. Lou?

You Knew?

Betty Lou and Mr. Hoo,

that's who!

But who's Hoo, and what's he do?

I haven't a clue!

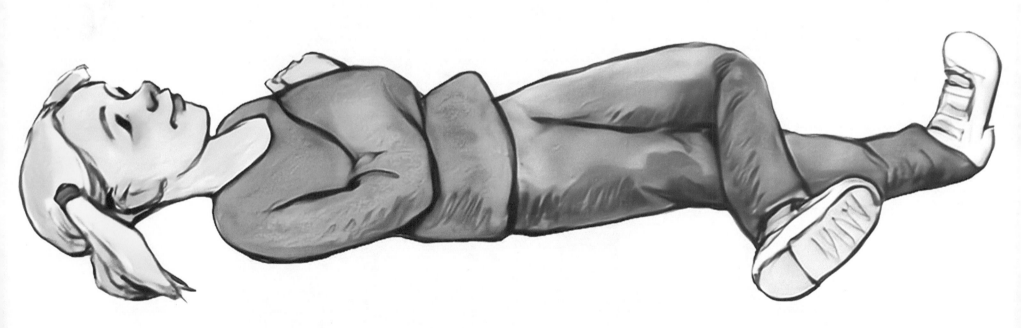

Hoo and Lou

have a brew

from the Sioux.

A Hudu brew,

that's how Hoo knew!

What Hoo knew?

I will tell it to you. Hoo knew…

Tutu on Fu-Fu

means woo-woo.

Hoo knew!!??

Ju-ju on new shoe

is a fruity goo.

Hoo knew!!??

Blue kangaroo poo is zoo news.

Hoo knew!!??

Achoo in caribou stew is…

Ewwww! Hoo knew!!??

Boo-boo on Babyboo leaves a lulu.

Hoo knew!!??

Cuckoo makes moo-moo and cock-a-doodle-do.

Hoo knew!!??

Overdue kazoo review

leaves avenue askew.

Hoo knew!!??

Fu Manchu shampoo grew

into Kung Fu hairdo.

Hoo knew!!??

Drew can't undo cockatoo tattoo in Oahu.

Hoo knew!!??

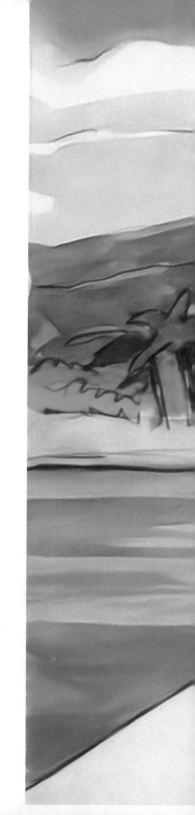

Buckaroo withdrew from

cordon bleu chew.

Parlez-vous?

Hoo knew!!??

Honeydew fondue overdo

gives number two. Hoo knew!!??

Phew!!!

About the Author

Bob Baumert is a recently retired electrical engineer who designed and developed computer circuitry and was granted seven patents in digital communications.

Looking for an outlet for his creative side, this is his first children's book. *Hoo Knew*?! is the opening storybook in his series, "Who, What, When, Where, Why, How."

"I enjoy reading out loud to my grandchildren, so the books are fun, both for the reader and the child following along with each illustrated scene in the story," Bob shared.

On the drawing board is the second book in the series, *Watt An Idea*!, about a brilliant light bulb full of fun new ideas.

About the Illustrator

Mark Bockrath lives in West Chester, Pennsylvania, where he works as a conservator of paintings in his private practice. He taught classes in painting materials and in figure painting at the Pennsylvania Academy of the Fine Arts and other art schools. His work is in numerous private and corporate collections, as well as at the U.S. Department of State.

Working mostly in pastel and oil, especially landscapes of Pennsylvania and Maine, *Hoo Knew*?! is Mark's first foray into book illustration. This interest was fostered by the many illustrated books he read as a child.

Acknowledgements

To all those who played a role in encouraging me and helping me bring this book to fruition…

To my children and especially my wife for all the suggestions and critiques…

And to my lifelong friend Mark Bockrath for climbing on board to contribute his outstanding illustrations…

I thank you!

CPSIA information can be obtained
at www.ICGtesting.com
Printed in the USA
LVHW010122141122
733042LV00009B/92